How To Use Video Modeling and Video Prompting

PRO-ED Series on Autism Spectrum Disorders

Edited by Richard L. Simpson

Titles in the Series

How To Develop and Implement Visual Supports

How To Do Discrete Trial Training

How To Do Incidental Teaching

How To Plan a Structured Classroom

How To Support Children with Problem Behavior

How To Teach Social Skills and Plan for Peer Social Interactions

How To Use Augmentative and Alternative Communication

How To Use Joint Action Routines

How To Use Video Modeling and Video Prompting

How To Write and Implement Social Scripts

HOW TO USE
VIDEO MODELING
AND
VIDEO PROMPTING

Jeff Sigafoos

Mark O'Reilly

Berenice de la Cruz

pro·ed
An International Publisher

8700 Shoal Creek Boulevard
Austin, Texas 78757-6897
800/897-3202 Fax 800/397-7633
www.proedinc.com

© 2007 by PRO-ED, Inc.
8700 Shoal Creek Boulevard
Austin, Texas 78757-6897
800/897-3202   Fax 800/397-7633
www.proedinc.com

Library of Congress Cataloging-in-Publication Data

Sigafoos, Jeff.
    How to use video modeling and video prompting / Jeff Sigafoos, Mark O'Reilly,
Berenice de la Cruz.
       p. cm. — (PRO-ED series on autism spectrum disorders)
    Includes bibliographical references.
    ISBN 1-4164-0152-0
    1. Autism in children. 2. Autistic children—Education. 3. Visual
programming (Computer science)   I. O'Reilly, Mark.   II. De La Cruz, Berenice.
III. Title.   IV. Series.
RJ506.A9S532 2006
649'.154—dc22

                        2006012499
                        CIP

Art Director: Jason Crosier
Designer: Nancy McKinney
This book is designed in Nexus Serif TF and Neutra Text.

Printed in the United States of America

1   2   3   4   5   6   7   8   9   10   10   09   08   07   06

Contents

Contents

About Autism Spectrum Disorders

Autism spectrum disorders (ASD) are complex, neurologically based developmental disabilities that typically appear early in life. The Autism Society of America (2004) estimates that as many as 1.5 million people in the United States have autism or some form of pervasive developmental disorder. Indeed, its prevalence makes ASD an increasingly common and currently the fastest-growing developmental disability. ASD are perplexing and enigmatic. According to the *Diagnostic and Statistical Manual of Mental Disorders,* individuals with ASD have difficulty in interacting normally with others; exhibit speech, language, and communication difficulties (e.g., delayed speech, echolalia); insist on routines and environmental uniformity; engage in self-stimulatory and stereotypic behaviors; and respond atypically to sensory stimuli (American Psychiatric Association, 2000; Simpson & Myles, 1998). In some cases, aggressive and self-injurious behavior may be present in these individuals. Yet, in tandem with these characteristics, children with ASD often have normal patterns of physical growth and development, a wide range of cognitive and language capabilities, and some individuals with ASD have highly developed and unique abilities (Klin, Volkmar, & Sparrow, 2000). These widely varied characteristics necessitate specially designed interventions and strategies orchestrated by knowledgeable and skilled professionals.

Preface to the Series

Teaching and managing learners with ASD can be demanding, but favorable outcomes for children and youth with autism and autism-related disabilities depend on professionals using appropriate and valid methods in their education. Because identifying and correctly using effective teaching methods is often enormously challenging (National Research Council, 2001; Simpson et al., 2005), it is the intent of this series to provide professionals with scientifically based methods for intervention. Each book in the series is designed to assist professionals and parents in choosing and correctly using a variety of interventions that have the potential to produce significant benefits for children and youth with ASD. Written in a user-friendly, straightforward fashion by qualified and experienced professionals, the books are aimed at individuals who seek practical solutions and strategies for successfully working with learners with ASD.

Richard L. Simpson
Series Editor

References

American Psychiatric Association. (2000). *Diagnostic and statistical manual of mental disorders* (4th ed., text rev.). Washington, DC: Author.

Autism Society of America. (2004). *What is autism?* Retrieved March 11, 2005, from http://autism-society.org

Klin, A., Volkmar, F., & Sparrow, S. (2000). *Asperger syndrome.* New York: Guilford Press.

National Research Council. (2001). *Educating children with autism.* Committee on Educational Interventions for Children with Autism, Division of Behavioral and Social Sciences and Education. Washington, DC: National Academy Press.

Simpson, R., de Boer-Ott, S., Griswold, D., Myles, B., Byrd, S., Ganz, J., et al. (2005). *Autism spectrum disorders: Interventions and treatments for children and youth.* Thousand Oaks, CA: Corwin Press.

Simpson, R. L., & Myles, B. S. (1998). *Educating children and youth with autism: Strategies for effective practice.* Austin, TX: PRO-ED.

Video modeling and video prompting can be used successfully to teach learners with autism spectrum disorders (ASD). Indeed, parents and teachers can use video modeling and video prompting to teach a variety of adaptive behaviors, which would allow individuals with ASD to participate more successfully in home, school, and community settings and enjoy a higher quality of life.

This step-by-step manual is intended for parents, teachers, staff, and therapists who are responsible for the care, education, and therapy of individuals with ASD. It provides details on how to make effective instructional videos and describes the steps involved in using video-based instruction to model and prompt desired behaviors and teach new skills. It also explains how to reduce dependence on video models and video prompts once the learner has acquired the desired behaviors.

Individuals with ASD often have difficulty learning many of the skills required to function effectively in home, school, and the community. Their deficits in adaptive behavior are usually evident in several major life areas, including self-care, daily living, academic, communication/language, and social-skills domains. Some learners with ASD may also have behavioral problems, such as aggression, self-injury, or tantrums, that can hinder their participation in society and interfere with mutually beneficial interpersonal relationships. Unlike their typically developing peers, learners with ASD often require highly specialized instruction to acquire new skills and learn appropriate ways of interacting with others. It is therefore not surprising that educational programs for learners with ASD place a heavy emphasis on teaching new skills and developing appropriate behaviors.

Teaching learners with ASD can be difficult and often requires careful use of specialized procedures. Fortunately, researchers have developed a number of effective procedures. The educational outcomes for learners with ASD are better when parents, teachers, staff, and therapists make use of research-based teaching procedures. Video modeling and video prompting are two research-based procedures that have proven successful in teaching learners with ASD.

When used properly, video modeling and video prompting can be highly effective in improving behavior and teaching a range of useful skills to learners with ASD. The types of skills that have been taught using these methods include self-care, daily living, play, communication, vocational, and social. Video modeling and video prompting can help educators to provide consistent instruction and thus ensure more efficient and effective skill acquisition and maintenance.

Because teaching learners with ASD can be difficult, parents, teachers, staff, and therapists may benefit from detailed guidelines on how to use proven procedures such as video modeling and video prompting. This manual describes the steps involved in using video modeling and video prompting in educational programs for learners with ASD and related developmental disabilities. This information is intended to help you make better use of video-based instructional procedures for teaching new skills and developing more appropriate behavior in learners with ASD.

Throughout the manual the reader will find a number of Review Exercises. These exercises are intended to facilitate your study of the material. They also provide an opportunity to consider how you might apply some of the concepts and information presented here.

Video modeling is a procedure in which a learner is shown a videotape of a model performing a target behavior or completing a desired task. The videotape is shown to the learner at the beginning of each teaching opportunity or session. After viewing the entire videotape—from start to finish—the learner is given the opportunity to perform the modeled behavior or complete the task that was demonstrated in the videotape. Usually, it is necessary to conduct several sessions—one or two per day for several days—before the learner will consistently perform the target behavior at a high level of proficiency.

A study by Rehfeldt, Dahman, Young, Cherry, and Davis (2003) illustrates the application of video modeling for teaching daily living skills. In this study, the authors focused on teaching three adult learners with developmental disabilities to make a sandwich. They first made a videotape that showed a different adult (not one of the participants) making a sandwich. To make a sandwich, the model followed a written task analysis (see "Step 3: Writing a Script or Developing a Task Analysis"), which listed a sequence of 17 steps for making a sandwich (e.g., get the bread out of the refrigerator; get the peanut butter from the counter). Learners were told to watch the video prior to each teaching session. After watching the entire video, learners were taken to a kitchen and given the opportunity to make a sandwich. The results showed that this video modeling procedure was associated with an increase in the percentage of steps completed correctly. Within three to seven sessions, all three learners were performing 100% of the steps correctly.

This study illustrates the three key features of video modeling:

1. The videotape shows a model performing a desired behavior or completing a task following a script or written task analysis. The model could be the parent or teacher, an actor, or a peer. In some cases, learners themselves serve as the models, which is known as video self-modeling (Sherer, Pierce, & Paredes, 2001). Guidelines for selecting models will be explained later, when we describe how to make instructional videotapes. (See "Step 5: Making the Instructional Video.")
2. The learner is shown the videotape prior to each teaching session. Some learners might have to be prompted to watch the

videotape as it is played. Effective prompts include a verbal instruction (e.g., "Watch this"), pointing to the screen where the video is playing, and orienting the learner to face the screen. Reinforcement, such as praise statements (e.g., "Good job. Keep watching.") or access to a preferred object, may also be necessary to ensure that the learner watches the entire videotape.

3. After watching the entire videotape, the learner is provided with an opportunity to perform the behavior or complete the task. The learner may need to receive several such sessions over a period of 5 to 10 days before learning the target behavior.

As another example, Nikopoulos and Keenan (2004) used video modeling to teach play skills to three children with autism. The instructional videotape showed a typically developing peer entering the playroom with an adult. The peer modeled the following target behaviors: (a) approaching the adult; (b) saying, "Let's play"; and (c) engaging in reciprocal toy play with the adult. After watching this video, the learner was taken into the playroom with the adult present. The results showed that this video modeling procedure was associated with an increase in the target behaviors for all three learners with autism. They watched the videotape prior to each daily play session and after a few days of this showed consistent learning in that they began to independently perform the target behaviors that were modeled in the videotape.

REVIEW EXERCISE 1

Reread the above paragraph, which provides a summary of the Nikopoulos and Keenan (2004) study. Underline the target behaviors that were modeled in the instructional videotape.

Answers: The target behaviors are: (a) approaching the adult, (b) saying, "Let's play," and (c) engaging in reciprocal toy play with the adult.

What Is Video Prompting?

Video prompting is a variation of video modeling. With video prompting, the learner is shown a series of video clips in sequence. It begins by showing the learner a video clip depicting only the first target behavior or only the first step in a task analysis. After watching the first video clip, the learner is given the opportunity to perform that behavior or complete that first step of a task. After that opportunity, the learner is shown the next video clip in the sequence and so on until all of the target behaviors have been shown. Showing the next clip in the series does not necessarily depend on the learner achieving success on the previous step. While that is the anticipated outcome, during the initial sessions the teacher may have to help the learner complete the step correctly so that the next clip in the sequence can be shown.

The main difference between video modeling and video prompting is that video modeling involves showing the entire videotape, whereas video prompting involves breaking the videotape into segments or clips and showing those one at a time.

To illustrate, Sigafoos et al. (2005) used video prompting to teach three adults with developmental disabilities to make microwave popcorn. The procedure involved showing a video clip of only one step of the task and then providing an opportunity to complete that step. A video clip showing the next step of the task was then presented and so forth until all 10 steps of the task analysis had been prompted. Each day for several days, the learners received one session of video prompting, which required about 10 minutes. The learners viewed the clips individually in a one-to-one format (Duker, Didden, & Sigafoos, 2004). That is, they went through one complete viewing of the video clips. After a few such sessions with this procedure, two of the three adults acquired the task and continued to perform 80% to 100% of the steps correctly when video prompting was withdrawn and at a 10-week follow-up.

REVIEW EXERCISE 2

Describe the main difference between video modeling and video prompting.

Answer: Video modeling involves showing the entire videotape, whereas video prompting involves breaking the videotape into segments or clips and showing them one at a time.

3

Video Modeling and Video Prompting Compared to Other Procedures

As mentioned in the introduction, the acquisition of new skills and the development of appropriate behaviors are major educational priorities for learners with ASD. Those priorities can be achieved using a range of direct instructional procedures that require instructor-directed training rather than the use of video technology. With instructor-delivered or -directed training, the instructor is present and offers instructional cues, delivers response prompts, corrects any errors that the learner might make, and provides reinforcement as necessary during each teaching session. Duker et al. (2004) provided a detailed description of instructor-directed training procedures and how they can be used to teach a variety of target behaviors (e.g., communication, imitation, social skills, daily living skills) to individuals with ASD and other developmental disabilities.

While instructor-directed training can be highly effective, it also has some potential disadvantages. Success often depends on maintaining a high degree of structure and consistency, which requires a considerable amount of instructor expertise. For example, the instructor must know how to create discrete trial learning opportunities that include presentation of discriminative stimuli. Once a stimulus has been presented, the instructor must wait a predetermined period of time (e.g., 5–10 seconds) to allow the learner to respond. During the wait period, it is critical to ensure that an incorrect response does not occur and that the opportunity ends with the learner making the correct response. This often requires implementing a carefully sequenced combination of response and stimulus prompts. To promote independence, those prompts will later have to be systematically faded.

Besides requiring a considerable amount of instructor expertise, instructor-directed training can be rather labor intensive. Thus, it can be difficult to implement with the skill and consistency necessary to ensure that learning occurs.

Video modeling and video prompting have at least four potential advantages over the use of instructor-directed training. First, implementation of video modeling or video prompting does not require the same amount of instructional expertise as the more direct instructional procedures described by Duker et al. (2004) often do. Using video technology for instruction does require some expertise in the technology itself, but the necessary skills are relatively easily to master and are not subject to the same nuances that arise in the give-and-take of instructor-directed training.

Second, it may be easier to ensure instructional consistency with video-based materials. Once an instructional video has been made, it can be played and replayed in the same way, thus ensuring consistency and avoiding any variation in the content and delivery of instruction from session to session.

Third, video modeling and video prompting may be less labor intensive than direct instruction. Once a model has been videotaped, for example, there may be no need for a highly skilled trainer to be present to model and prompt the desired behavior prior to or during each teaching session.

Fourth, even though there is some initial expense for the purchase of a video camera and monitor, the same equipment can be used to create and present instructional materials for a vast number of skills and behaviors. Thus over time, as the video library grows, there should be considerable savings in time investment. That savings means that parents, teachers, and therapists would have more time to engage the learner in other life experiences.

We are not proposing that you use only instructor-delivered training *or* video modeling or prompting. These methods of providing instruction are not mutually exclusive and can often be combined to enhance the teaching process and promote better learning. There is no reason the response prompts, error correction techniques, and reinforcement procedures used with instructor-delivered training cannot be used in conjunction with video modeling and video prompting. In fact, an instructor will often have to provide some direct instruction—such as delivering additional response prompts, correcting errors, and providing contingent reinforcement—even when using video modeling and video prompting, to boost the effectiveness of the video procedure.

REVIEW EXERCISE 3

List four potential advantages to video modeling or video prompting compared to instructor-directed training.

Answers: (1) Does not require as much expertise; (2) easier to ensure consistency; (3) not as labor intensive; and (4) cost and time savings.

Types of Learners Who Benefit from Video Modeling and Video Prompting

Video modeling and video prompting have been used with learners of various ages and with varying types and degrees of disability. It has been used successfully with preschool- and elementary school–aged children, adolescents, and adults. Even children as young as 3 years have benefited from video-based instruction (Dauphin, Kinney, & Stromer, 2004). However, it would probably be difficult to use video modeling or video prompting successfully with infants, who have yet to learn to imitate or orient and attend to models.

Video modeling and video prompting have been used with learners with varying types of disability, including ASD, attention-deficit/hyperactivity disorder, behavior disorder, developmental delay, learning disability, and severe to profound mental retardation. Lack of speech or language or having a low level of intellectual ability does not seem to necessarily prevent a learner from benefiting from video modeling or video prompting; learners with no speech or language and those with mental ages as low as 2 years have learned new skills through the use of these techniques.

So far, there is little research on whether some learners might be better suited to video-based instructional procedures than others. Such procedures would seem more likely to be effective with learners who already have some level of imitative ability and can already attend to and learn from watching others. Thus, video prompting and video modeling are probably best suited to learners who have demonstrated the ability to learn through observation. Indeed, the ability to imitate an observed model could be considered a prerequisite for the use of video modeling and video prompting. If the learner has not yet developed the ability to imitate or demonstrated the ability to acquire new skills through observing a model, those skills could be taught using the types of instructor-delivered training procedures described by Duker et al. (2004).

Steps in Using Video Modeling and Video Prompting

The process of using video modeling or video prompting for teaching individuals with ASD involves a number of steps, which should be completed systematically and in a logical sequence. This chapter describes each of those steps. Completing the steps in the order given here should enable you to make effective use of video-based instructional procedures for teaching new skills and developing more appropriate behavior in learners with ASD.

Step 1: Selecting Target Behaviors

As mentioned in the introduction, numerous skills and behaviors have been taught or improved using video modeling and video prompting. The specific skill or behavior that becomes the focus of teaching is known as the target behavior. For example, a mother might want to teach her son how to independently dress for school in the morning. Dressing for school would thus be the target behavior. As another example, a secondary-school home economics teacher might want his students to learn how to wash their dirty plates, utensils, and cups after lunch. Washing dishes would be the target behavior.

When identifying behaviors to target for instruction, it is helpful to specify precisely what you want the learner to do. Target behaviors should be described so that they are observable and measurable. Making a sandwich is observable and so is applying sunscreen, but being angry or cooperating are not good target behaviors. More precise behaviors that constitute anger or cooperation would need to be specified. Target behaviors related to anger might be swearing and throwing objects. For cooperation, the target behavior might be specified as sharing toys with peers.

Table 1 lists a number of target behaviors that have been taught using video modeling or video prompting. These target behaviors have been grouped into the following areas: self-care, daily living, communication, social and academic, and vocational skills.

TABLE 1
Examples of Target Behaviors by Domain

Self-care	Daily living	Communication	Social and academic	Vocational
Brushing teeth	Making a sandwich	Answering questions	Playing with toys	Operating video player
Washing face	Using a microwave	Naming emotions	Spelling	Mailing a letter
Exiting to fire alarm	Washing dishes	Giving compliments	Playing tag	Caring for a pet
Making the bed	Putting away groceries	Requesting preferred objects	Following a schedule	Sweeping the floor
Cleaning eye glasses	Setting the table	Making conversation	Reducing tantrums	Emptying trash
Dressing	Grocery shopping	Asking another to play	Increasing on-task behavior	Cleaning office

REVIEW EXERCISE 4

In the following examples, underline the words that specify the target behavior:

1. Roberto is being taught to purchase a list of grocery items from a supermarket.
2. Juliet frequently approaches her peers too closely and stares at them or hits them. The teacher wants Juliet to learn more appropriate social skills. The teacher decides to first teach Juliet to approach peers to 1 yard away and then ask if she can play with them.
3. Andrew is learning to live in the community. As part of this, he has to learn to be more responsible. Staff in his community home are therefore teaching him to lock his front door when leaving home for the day.
4. Darci's father wants to teach her to enjoy recreational activities with the family. He often takes the family to a lake to camp and fish and would like Darci to participate in the activities of these family outings. One such activity is to spend some time each morning trying to catch some fish. He wants to teach her to enjoy this activity.

Answers: You are on the right track if you underlined (1) purchase a list of grocery items, (2) approach peers to 1 yard and ask if she can play, and (3) lock the front door. Identifying the target behavior for Darci is more difficult because enjoying fishing is not easily observable and measurable and the act of fishing involves a number of interrelated responses. This target behavior is too vague and needs to be more clearly specified. For example, instruction might begin by teaching Darci how to cast a lure and reel it in.

Step 2: Getting the Right Equipment

Making use of video modeling and video prompting requires two pieces of equipment. To make the instructional video, you must have a video camera. To play the videotape, you must have a videotape player and monitor. Various brands and models of both cameras and video players and monitors are available. Standard VCR-based cameras and players are becoming obsolete, although they are still available and relatively inexpensive. It is worth considering the added expense of a digital video camera. One advantage of digital video is that the clips can be downloaded to a computer and shown with commercially available software, such as Windows Media Player or RealPlayer.

Step 3: Writing a Script or Developing a Task Analysis

Creating an instructional video is similar to making a movie. As in movie making, it helps to start by having a script or a detailed storyboard that lays out the movie scene by scene. For an instructional video, the script might consist of a written narrative that describes what the model will do and say. The script for teaching the learner to perform a multistep task might take the form of a written task analysis, showing the sequence of steps the learner will need to follow to successfully complete the task.

Writing a Script

The script that specifies what the model should do during the filming may be fairly simple or more elaborate. A script for teaching social initiation,

11

for example, might simply show the model approaching a peer and asking, "Can I play with you?" Other target behaviors, such as sociodramatic play or conversational turn-taking would seem to require more elaborate scripts, given that more target behaviors may need to be modeled and may need to occur in a certain order or sequence.

Regardless of the complexity of the target task, it is important to have a script that will guide the making of the video. The script does not have to be a word-by-word transcript or a highly detailed description of the skill or interaction you are trying to teach. Instead, it could consist of a general outline of the interaction or a general description of what should happen. Avoiding too much detail may facilitate generalization, in that the person watching may learn what *types* of behaviors to engage in rather than merely learning to rehash a detailed script by rote. As an example, Sherer and her colleagues (2001) developed a script for teaching conversation skills to children with autism. The script listed a series of conversational turns between an adult and a peer model. A brief conversation might be scripted as follows:

ADULT: Hi, Jody. What are you planning for your afternoon?
PEER MODEL: I'm going for a swim at the pool. What about you?
ADULT: I am going to a movie.
PEER MODEL: Really? What movie are you going to see?
ADULT: That new James Bond movie.

As another example, here is a script for answering the telephone: The script begins with a telephone ringing. After the second ring, the model—who happens to be a same-aged peer—walks over to the telephone, picks it up, and says, "Hello." The caller, who can be heard but not seen, says, "Hi. Can I speak with your mother?" The peer-model says, "Yes, I will get her. Hang on." He then calls out for his mother ("Mom, there is a call for you.") and hands her the telephone as she approaches.

Developing a Task Analysis

If you plan to teach a skill that involves a sequence of several responses, such as making toast or washing a car, the script is best written as a task analysis. *Task analysis* is the process of breaking a task into its component steps. It is important to ensure that a task analysis follows a logical sequence and does not omit any necessary steps. Thus, when a task analysis is being written, it is helpful for one person to perform the task while another writes down each step that needs to be completed in the proper sequence. The number of steps in a particular task analysis may vary depending on the learner's abilities. Table 2 provides an example of a task analysis that can be used for teaching a person to make a salad.

TABLE 2
Task Analysis for Making a Salad

Steps in the Task Analysis

1. Take the bag of lettuce out of the refrigerator.
2. Retrieve the salad bowl from the counter.
3. Open the bag of lettuce and put the lettuce into the bowl.
4. Select one tomato from the cupboard.
5. Wash the tomato under the faucet in the sink.
6. Dry the tomato with a paper towel.
7. Retrieve the cutting board from the cupboard.
8. Select a knife from the utensil drawer.
9. Place the tomato on the board and slice it into four segments.
10. Put the four tomato segments into the salad bowl.
11. Retrieve the salad dressing from the refrigerator.
12. Open the salad dressing and sprinkle some into the salad bowl.
13. Select the salad fork and spoon from the utensil drawer.
14. Use the salad fork and spoon to mix the dressing into the salad.
15. Using the salad fork and spoon, put one serving onto a plate.
16. Obtain a fork from the utensil drawer.
17. Take the plate to the table and eat the salad with the fork.

Step 4: Obtaining Baseline Data

The intervention process begins with the collection of baseline data. *Baseline* refers to the status of the learner's performance before she receives any instruction. Before you use video modeling or video prompting, it would be useful to obtain baseline data to find out how well the learner currently performs the target behavior or completes the designated task.

Baseline data could reveal that the learner can already perform some of the scripted behaviors or some of the steps in the task analysis. In such cases, the instructional videotape would not need to cover the entire script or task analysis but could focus instead on those specific aspects of the script or task analysis that are proving difficult for the learner. When the baseline data indicate that the learner performs little of the target task, the instructional videotape should model all of the scripted behaviors or steps in the task analysis.

Figure 1 shows baseline data for Renee, a 14-year-old learner with ASD. Because Renee liked to eat salads—consisting of lettuce, tomato, and vinaigrette dressing—her parents thought it would be a good idea to teach her how to make her own salad. They first ran 5 days of baseline following the task analysis shown in Table 2. For each baseline session, Renee was brought to the kitchen and asked to make a salad. All of the materials necessary to make a salad were available in the kitchen. After giving the verbal instruction, her mother or father allowed Renee 10 minutes to complete the task and recorded which steps in the task analysis she performed correctly.

As shown in the data in Figure 1, Renee consistently completed steps 1 and 2 of the task (taking the bag of lettuce out of the refrigerator and retrieving the salad bowl from the counter). In sessions 2, 3, and 4, she also completed step 3 (opening the bag of lettuce and putting it into the bowl). Clearly, she could do some of the task, but the data indicate that she needed to learn how to do steps 4 through 17, although sometimes she might also need help with step 3. Her parents decided to teach those steps using video prompting. They planned to start the video prompting procedure on day 6 because the baseline indicated a clear and stable pattern of performance.

Step 5: Making the Instructional Video

Four decisions need to be made with respect to making instructional video-tapes: (a) Which aspects of the script or steps in the task analysis are to be filmed? (b) Who will serve as the model in the videotape? (c) From which perspective will the videotape be filmed? (d) Should you include voice-over instructions?

Deciding Which Aspects To Film

As Renee's example illustrates, baseline data can help pinpoint which behaviors in a script or steps in a task analysis are crucial to include in the instructional video. Once that has been determined, those aspects of the script or task analysis are filmed using the video camera. If the baseline data show that the learner does not do any parts of the script or task analysis correctly, the entire script or task analysis should be filmed. Sometimes baseline data are highly variable and thus difficult to interpret. By "variable," we mean that the learner's performance on the task may be inconsistent and vary in terms of percent correct from session to session.

For example, Luke may perform steps 1 and 2 correctly the first time baseline data are taken but, when subsequent baseline data are taken, fail to perform steps 1 and 2 correctly and instead perform steps 3 and 4 correctly.

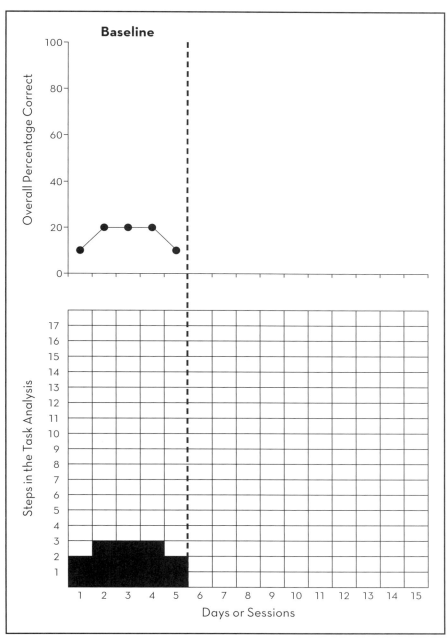

FIGURE 1. Renee's data across 5 baseline sessions. The top panel shows the overall percentage of steps completed correctly. The bottom panel indicates which specific steps in the task analysis were completed correctly (■) or incorrectly (□).

After a couple more baseline points have been taken, it is still not clear which steps, if any, Luke is really able to perform. In such a case, it is probably best to film the entire script or every step in the task analysis. Because you want to ensure that the learner acquires the skill to perform the target behavior, it is important to make sure the teaching process is systematic, and that will mean including all of the steps in the video (unless the learner is consistently performing some of the steps already).

Selecting a Model

Various individuals can be used as the models or actors when making the instructional video (Ayres & Langone, 2005). Effective models have included parents, teachers, peers, residential staff, and unfamiliar trainers. In some cases, as mentioned previously, the learner serves as his own model, a procedure known as video self-modeling (Buggey, 2005). Self-modeling can be very effective, but you have to somehow ensure that the learner can be filmed engaging in the correct behaviors. This can be difficult if the learner does not already possess the required behaviors or skills. One way to do it is to assist the individual using verbal and gesture prompts or physical guidance and then edit the prompts from the videotape.

Whether the actor is self or other, familiar or unfamiliar, peer or parent, teacher or trainer appears to make little difference to the overall effectiveness of video modeling or video prompting (Buggey, 2005; Sherer et al., 2001). It is probably more critical to ensure that the actor demonstrates the required behaviors in a way that will be easy for the learner to observe and imitate. This will require finding an actor who can demonstrate the required behaviors clearly and slowly but fluently. Of course, some scripts are probably best modeled by certain types of people to enhance the ecological validity of the instructional video. Thus, if the scripts used in the instructional video mimic situations in the "real world," the skills taught will be more likely to be generalized to the real world. For example, if your aim were to develop better peer interactions, it would make sense to use peer models. On the other hand, if your aim were to teach the learner to initiate a conversation at home, siblings and parents could be the models.

Selecting the Perspective

Instructional videotapes can be filmed from one of two perspectives: spectator or participant. Both perspectives have been successfully used in instructional videotapes for individuals with ASD. It is unclear whether one perspective might be better suited to some behaviors or some individuals.

For video modeling, the videotape is most often filmed from the perspective of a spectator watching someone perform the target behavior. The learner assumes the role of a spectator and watches the model as one would watch an actor on television. For example, when teaching a learner to set a table, the video might be filmed to show the model first picking up the placemat from a side table and placing it on the table and then completing each subsequent step in the task until the entire task has been filmed.

Video prompts, in contrast, have sometimes been filmed from the perspective of the participant, the so-called subjective viewpoint (Norman, Collins, & Schuster, 2001). From this perspective, the learner sees the step or behavior being completed from the perspective of the performer completing the task, not the perspective of a spectator watching someone else complete the task. For example, when filming a task such as table setting from this perspective, the initial video clip might consist of an over-the-shoulder shot of the performer's two hands picking up the placemat and placing it on the table. This perspective shows the target behavior as it would appear to the learner when she is subsequently given the opportunity to perform it. Thus, there is presumably a closer match between what the learner sees in the video and what the learner will see when she is engaged in the target behavior herself. This may be an advantage for learners who have difficultly seeing things from another's perspective.

Including Spoken Instructions

Video enables you to record sounds and speech as well as visual movement. When teaching social skills, for example, it is equally important to see the visual (a child approaching a peer) and hear the verbal (the child saying, "Hello, Meghan, how are you today?"). When the target behavior includes speech, it obviously makes sense to include that when filming the script.

Other activities or tasks do not always involve or require much sound or speech. If you are filming someone washing dishes, for example, the model does not necessarily have to say anything. However, specific voice-over instructions can be included. Consider the previous example of a video clip filmed for teaching the first step of setting a table. We said the visual part of the video might consist of an over-the-shoulder shot of the performer's two hands picking up the placemat and placing it on the table. To that, one might add the voice-over instruction: "First, put down the placemat." Thus, when a learner watches that video clip, he not only will see the target behavior but will also be given a verbal prompt of what to do. Adding voice-over instructions will probably enhance the videotape and make it a more effective teaching tool. Voice-over instructions should be clear and state precisely what the learner is supposed to do or say.

For some learners, spoken instructions alone, known as auditory prompting, may be sufficient for teaching the target behaviors (Witt & Wacker, 1981). It is also possible that a combination of visual and auditory information in an instructional video could be detrimental for some

17

learners if they are overly selective in their attention (Dunlap, Koegel, & Burk, 1981). To date, no studies have specifically investigated the effects of including voice-over instructions with video modeling or prompting. In our research, we have always included voice-over instructions. Although we cannot say for sure that voice-over instruction has made the prompts more effective, its inclusion does not appear to have caused any problems. In our experience, the use of voice-over instruction along with video models has proven to be effective.

Step 6: Arranging the Teaching Environment

The instructional environment should be arranged to facilitate teaching and learning. This is especially important during the initial teaching sessions. Creating a well-organized and structured teaching environment is likely to improve the ease and speed of learning.

Parents, teachers, and therapists should consider three factors when arranging the teaching environment. First, it is important to designate a specific time for running teaching sessions. Ideally, sessions should occur daily and at the same time each day. To increase the applied relevance of the program, sessions can be scheduled at times when the target behaviors would be expected to occur. If you are teaching the learner to dress, for example, sessions could occur in the morning after the learner has showered. If you are teaching the learner to wash dishes, sessions could occur after meals. Sometimes, however, it may be better to conduct sessions immediately prior to the opportunity to use the target behavior, rather than at the same time. For example, it may be better to use a video to model appropriate social skills immediately prior to the time when the learner will be interacting with peers, rather than at the same time peers are available for interaction, when the presence of the video could be distracting and might interfere with the social interaction.

Second, it is important to designate a specific place for conducting teaching sessions. As with the time, sessions can be scheduled in the same place the target behavior would be expected to occur to increase the applied relevance of the program. If you are teaching the learner to dress, sessions could occur in the learner's bedroom or perhaps in the bathroom. If you are teaching the learner to wash dishes, sessions could occur in the kitchen. In some situations, however, training might be better suited to a simulated environment where it is easier for the teacher to show the video and reduce distractions. It may be easier to do some initial instruction on grocery shopping using a video modeling procedure that is implemented in the classroom, rather than trying to provide video-based instruction in an actual grocery store. But because not all learners will be able to transfer what they have learned in the classroom to the grocery store, it is important to provide opportunities for learners to perform the skills outside of the simulated training environment, as well. And even if the learner cannot *watch* the video in the actual setting, filming it in the actual setting may be helpful, as it will make the video more realistic.

Although the learner might have to view the videotape in an unrelated setting, she should be given opportunities to perform the modeled target behavior in the actual setting. For example, the learner might have to sit in the classroom to watch a video that models appropriate playground behaviors, but after watching the videotape, the learner should be allowed to perform the modeled behaviors on the playground. The chances of the learner performing the modeled behaviors are perhaps greater if the videotape was filmed in the same playground setting.

Third, the materials used in the videotape should be the same materials that the learner would be expected to use when performing the target behavior in the actual environment. When filming a video for teaching microwave oven use, for example, it makes sense to film the model using the same microwave found in the learner's home. When filming a video for teaching dressing, it makes sense to film the model using the type of clothing that the learner would choose to wear. When filming a video for teaching grocery shopping, it makes sense to film in the grocery stores in the learner's neighborhood.

The basic principle considered in this section is that of embedded instruction. As in movies, it is generally better to film on location than in a studio. It is also usually better to create video content that reflects the learner's world in terms of times, locations, and materials. Doing so may facilitate generalization and maintenance of learning because the videotapes will be more realistic.

Step 7: Presenting Video Models and Video Prompts

To benefit from an instructional video, the learner must watch the videotape and attend to its relevant content. The way the video models or prompts are presented may influence learning. For some learners it may be sufficient to simply place the video player nearby, run the tape, and let them watch. For others, however, additional procedures may be required to ensure that the learner watches and attends to the videotape. Specifically, the learner may need to be prompted to watch and attend to the video. Here are some procedures that can be used for that purpose:

1. Make sure the video monitor is near the learner and that he has a clear and unobstructed view of it.

19

2. Remove distractions from the surrounding environment.

3. Immediately prior to playing the video, gain the learner's attention, point to the monitor, and say, "Watch this."

4. Praise the learner for remaining oriented to the video screen as the videotape is playing (e.g., "That's good. Keep watching").

5. If the learner looks away, remind him to keep watching. If necessary, gently orient him toward the video. This may require lightly turning his head to face the video monitor.

6. While the videotape is running, use your finger to point out relevant content and verbally describe the relevant behavior (e.g., "Look. The person is using the sponge to wash the plate").

It is important to keep in mind, however, that the use of these types of prompts could be distracting. Therefore, if you use prompts while the videotape is playing, it might be useful to then replay the videotape without using any prompts. By doing that, you will give the learner a chance to pick up details that he missed during the first viewing. In other words, repeated viewings can be helpful for students who need to be prompted to look at the video. For other students, watching the video once each session may be sufficient.

Step 8: Monitoring Progress

It is important to collect data on the learner's performance to determine whether the target behavior is improving as a result of using video modeling or video prompting. Prior to implementing video-based instruction, you should collect baseline data, as explained in step 4. Once the video modeling or video prompting procedure is started, you should continue to collect data during each session. The type of data collected and the method of collection should be the same as in baseline. This will allow you to compare the video-based instruction data with the baseline data, and the comparison will tell you whether the video procedure is working. If it is working, the data should look like those shown in Figure 2. Figure 2 is a continuation of the baseline data presented in Figure 1. As you can see, the video prompting procedure was started with session 6. Renee showed an immediate and rather large increase in the percentage of steps completed correctly. In fact, she reached and stayed at 100% correct after only five exposures to the video prompting procedure. Data shows that the video prompting procedure was effective in teaching Renee how to make a salad.

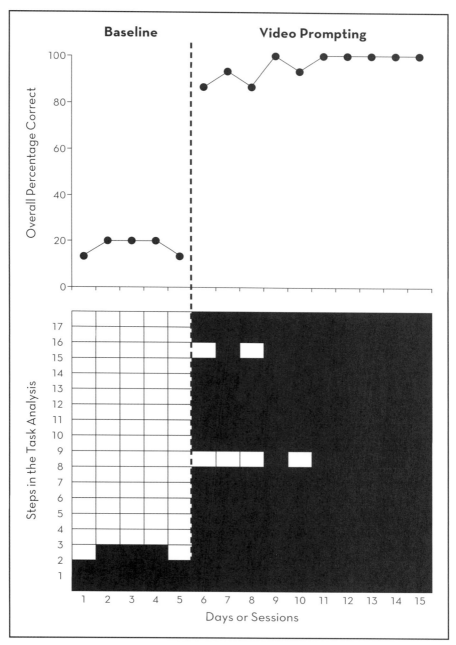

FIGURE 2. Renee's data across 5 baseline sessions and 10 sessions with video prompting. The top panel shows the overall percentage of steps completed correctly. The bottom panel indicates which specific steps in the task analysis were completed correctly (■) or incorrectly (□).

Step 9: Troubleshooting

Progress is not always as rapid or as large as shown in Figure 2. In some cases, the target behavior may not increase after video modeling or video prompting is introduced. In other cases, the behaviors may increase a little but not to an acceptable level. This is the situation illustrated in Figure 3. The data in Figure 3 are from Greg, a 15-year-old boy with ASD who was also being taught to make a salad. As the data illustrate, Greg did not perform any of the steps correctly during baseline (0% correct). When video prompting started, he made some improvement, in that he learned to do 10 of the steps correctly. His percentage of steps performed correctly increased from 0% in baseline to a high of 58% with video prompting. However, this meant that he did not learn to do nearly half of the steps correctly, and thus he was not able to make a salad independently.

As illustrated in Figure 3, when data are collected on the learner's performance during each session, lack of improvement will be obvious by simply looking at the graphed data. Improvement or progress is indicated when the graphed data show an increase in the target behavior, such as an increase in the number of steps that the learner performs correctly and independently. Generally, it can be expected that the learner will make steady progress within five to seven sessions.

Of course, there will be differences in the rate of learning for different students, but, as a general rule of thumb, if a learner does not show improvement, such as an increase in the percentage of steps completed independently, within five to seven sessions, parents, teachers, and therapists will need to troubleshoot or revise the program.

Troubleshooting involves searching out why the procedure might be failing and then refining it to address the problems. Once the problems have been identified, the program must be modified to address them and reimplemented to see if it will work better. Table 3 lists three common types of problems and possible solutions for each. In Greg's case, the problem appeared to be that some steps in the task analysis were too big and some were too small. His parents therefore rewrote the task analysis, creating a new set of 17 steps. In the new version, the steps that Greg was having trouble with were divided into smaller steps, and other steps were combined into larger steps. Each step in this restructured task analysis was then filmed and the procedure tried again, this time with success, as shown in Figure 3.

Another problem may be a lack of reinforcement. This occurs when performing the target behavior does not lead to a reinforcing consequence for the learner. A possible solution is to identify preferred stimuli that can function as reinforcers and deliver them to the learner as a reward for engaging in the target behavior. A third problem that may be encountered is that the learner may lack observational and imitative learning abilities.

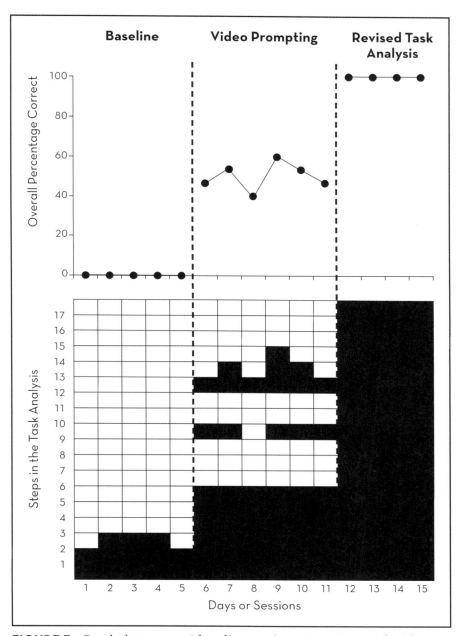

FIGURE 3. Greg's data across 5 baseline sessions, 6 sessions with video prompting, and 4 final sessions when video prompting was used with the revised task analysis. The top panel shows the overall percentage of steps completed correctly. The bottom panel indicates which specific steps in the task analysis were completed correctly (■) or incorrectly (□).

TABLE 3
Common Types of Problems and Possible Solutions

Description of problem	Possible solution
Lack of reinforcement. Performing the target behavior does not lead to a re-inforcing consequence for the learner.	Make sure performing the target behaviors leads to reinforcing consequences. Identify preferred stimuli that could function as reinforcers and deliver those to the learner for engaging in the target behavior.
Poor video content. The target behaviors are not shown clearly. The script is too complicated, or the steps in the task analysis are too big.	Rewrite the script or task analysis and then re-shoot the video. Make sure the target behaviors are modeled clearly and slowly.
Lack of prerequisites. The learner lacks observational and imitative learning abilities.	Video modeling and video prompting require learners who can learn by observation and imitation. If learners lack those abilities, they may show little progress with video modeling or prompting. Those skills should first be taught to the learner. It may also help to add instructor-directed training, including physical prompting and error correction, to the video procedure.

Possible solutions are to teach those skills and add instructor-directed training (e.g., physical prompting and error correction) to the video procedure.

Step 10: Fading Video Models and Video Prompts

The instructor must work toward eliminating the need for continued video modeling or video prompting to ensure that the learner does not become prompt dependent. Independence means that the learner will eventually perform the target behaviors correctly without having to be prompted. With some learners, the video can be removed without any detriment to the learner's performance after video modeling or video prompting has been used to teach the target behavior. Unfortunately, with other learners, abruptly withdrawing the instructional video can lead to a significant decrease in performance. This phenomenon is well documented in behavioral training programs for individuals with developmental disabilities that have used other types of instructional prompts, such as verbal instructions, gestures or pointing, and physical guidance (Duker et al., 2004). Consequently, when

24

TABLE 4
Procedures for Fading Video Models and Video Prompts

Procedure	Description
Delayed start or premature stop	Gradually show less and less of the video by either ending it prematurely or starting it a later point in the tape (e.g., 30 seconds into the tape, 2 minutes into the tape). This means that over several sessions the learner will be watching less and less of the video.
Error correction	Instead of showing the video prior to the sessions, show the relevant parts of the video only if the learner makes an error.
Scene fading	Gradually delete certain scenes of the script or certain steps of the task analysis. This process might begin with the steps that the learner mastered first.

prompts cannot be successfully eliminated abruptly, it is generally recommended that they be faded gradually.

There has been little research into procedures for fading video models or video prompts. However, one promising approach is known as *chunking* (Sigafoos et al., in press). Chunking can be used with video prompting, in which a separate video clip has been filmed for each step of the task. The chunking fading process involves gradually adding more steps to each video clip until all of the once separate clips have been merged into a single video. After that, it may be possible to remove the video prompting completely.

Other procedures for fading video models and prompts are described in Table 4. It is important to note that fading begins only after the learner has mastered the target behavior. Once the target behavior has been acquired with video modeling or video prompting, the aim is to maintain the behavior at mastery levels as the video models or prompts are gradually faded. Note that the procedures described in Table 4 have not yet been fully researched to determine if they would work for fading video models or video prompts.

Case Study on Using Video Modeling

Kimberly is an 11-year-old girl with autism. She has many deficits in adaptive behavior and functions in the moderate-to-severe range of intellectual disability. She lives at home with her mother, father, an older sister, and a younger brother. All of the children are expected to do some chores around the house. Her parents decided that Kimberly's chores would include setting the table for dinner. They decided to use video modeling to teach her how to set the table.

The first step involved writing a task analysis. The parents had a certain way in mind for how the table should be set. The steps they developed (see Table 5) were written together as they went through the motions of setting the table.

The next step was to collect baseline data to determine which if any of these steps Kimberly might already know how to do. They collected baseline data over three evening sessions. Each session was conducted in the dining room area just before their usual dinnertime. Kimberly was brought to the dining room, and her mother asked her to set the table. Using the task analysis as a data sheet, her mother recorded which steps in the task Kimberly

TABLE 5
Kimberly's Task Analysis for Setting the Table

Steps in the Task Analysis

1. Put a placemat on the table in front of each of the five chairs.
2. Put one dinner plate on top of each placemat.
3. Put a napkin on the table to the right of each plate.
4. Put one fork and one spoon on top of each napkin.
5. Put one knife to the left of each plate.
6. Put one water glass near the top left corner of each plate.
7. Put the bowl of dinner salad in the center of the table.
8. Put the wooden salad spoon and fork in the salad bowl.
9. Put the large plate containing the main meal on the table next to the salad bowl.
10. Call the family to dinner.

was able to complete. Kimberly was given 5 minutes to set the table. During baseline, Kimberly received no other prompts or assistance. The baseline phase needed to be done for only three evenings because Kimberly did not do any of the steps correctly. She always ended up with 0% correct. It was pretty clear after three sessions that Kimberly did not know how to set the table.

The third step was to make the instructional video. Each of the 10 steps of the task analysis was filmed in sequence as a single videotape, which showed the father doing step 1, then step 2, and so on, until all the steps had been completed in order and the table was set in line with the task analysis. The parents used a digital camera to make the videotape. Kimberly's mother filmed each clip from a spectator's perspective; when Kimberly watched the videotape, she would see each step being completed by her father. Verbal instructions were included in the videotape for each step of the task. For example, for step 1, as the father was putting the placemats on the table, the mother's voice could be heard saying, "First, put down the placemats. Put one placemat in front of each chair."

The next step was to begin the video modeling procedure. Each evening, Kimberly was brought to the dining room just before dinnertime. A computer was on a sideboard near the table. Kimberly's mother turned on the computer and pointed to it, saying, "Kimberly, watch this." Kimberly then watched the entire videotape. When the videotape ended, the mother said, "Okay, Kimberly, I want you to set the table, just like in the video."

Kimberly watched the video each evening prior to getting the chance to set the table. After a few such sessions, she was consistently doing 8 of the 10 steps correctly. However, she always made two errors. She would put the knife with the fork and spoon, and she put the water glass on the wrong side of the plate. Although those were technically errors, neither her mother nor her father was very concerned about them. Her parents thought they could tolerate those minor mistakes. They therefore decided to stop the training on setting the table and started using video modeling to teach Kimberly other new skills, such as helping vacuum the house and play games with her brother and sister. For the latter skill, they developed a script of how to say and do certain things for several play situations, such as playing hide-and-seek.

Video prompting and video modeling can be used to teach a variety of skills and improve a wide range of target behaviors. It is important to clearly specify the target behavior and develop a script or task analysis prior to creating the instructional video. The filmed version of the script or task analysis should show an appropriate model performing the target behavior clearly and slowly but fluently.

After baseline data has been collected, the learner is exposed to the video model or prompts, and the target behavior is monitored to see if there is improvement. If improvement does not occur, the procedure may need to be modified. This may require ensuring reinforcement, revising the script or task analysis, or adding additional prompting. Following acquisition, the target behaviors should maintain without the need for continued video modeling or video prompting. This may require implementing additional fading procedures.

By following the steps outlined in this manual, parents, teachers, and therapists should be able to design and implement a successful teaching program using video modeling or video prompting.

References

Ayres, K. M., & Langone, J. (2005). Intervention and instruction with video for students with autism: A review of the literature. *Education and Training in Developmental Disabilities, 40,* 183–196.

Buggey, T. (2005). Video self-modeling applications with students with autism spectrum disorder in a small private school setting. *Focus on Autism and Other Developmental Disabilities, 20,* 52–63.

Dauphin, M., Kinney, E. M., & Stromer, R. (2004). Using video-enhanced activity schedules and matrix training to teach sociodramatic play to a child with autism. *Journal of Positive Behavior Interventions, 6,* 238–250.

Duker, P. C., Didden, R., & Sigafoos, J. (2004). *One-to-one training: Instructional procedures for learners with developmental disabilities.* Austin, TX: PRO-ED.

Dunlap, G., Koegel, R. L., & Burke, J. C. (1981). Educational implications of stimulus overselectivity in autistic children. *Exceptional Education Quarterly, 2,* 37–49

Nikopoulos, C. K., & Keenan, M. (2004). Effects of video modeling on social initiations by children with autism. *Journal of Applied Behavior Analysis, 37,* 93–96.

Norman, J. M., Collins, B. C., & Schuster, J. W. (2001). Using an instructional package including video technology to teach self-help skills to elementary students with mental deficiency. *Journal of Special Education Technology, 16,* 5–18.

Rehfeldt, R. A., Dahman, D., Young, A., Cherry, H., & Davis, P. (2003). Teaching a simple meal preparation skill to adults with moderate and severe mental retardation using video modeling. *Behavioral Interventions, 18,* 209–218.

Sherer, M., Pierce, K. L., & Paredes, S. (2001). Enhancing conversation skills in children with autism via video technology: Which is better, "Self" or "Other" as a model? *Behavior Modification, 25,* 140–158.

Sigafoos, J., O'Reilly, M., Cannella, H., Edrisinha, C., de la Cruz, B., Upadhyaya, M., et al. (in press). Evaluation of a video prompting and fading procedure for teaching dish washing skills to adults with developmental disabilities. *Journal of Behavioral Education.*

Sigafoos, J., O'Reilly, M., Cannella, H., Upadhyaya, M., Edrisinha, C., Lancioni, G. E., et al. (2005). Computer-presented video prompting for teaching microwave oven use to three adults with developmental disabilities. *Journal of Behavioral Education, 14,* 189–201.

Witt, J. C., & Wacker, D. P. (1981). Teaching children to respond to auditory directives: An evaluation of two procedures. *Behavior Research of Severe Developmental Disabilities, 2,* 175–189.

Alcantara, P. R. (1994). Effects of videotape instructional package on purchasing skills of children with autism. *Exceptional Children, 61,* 40–56.

Apple, A. L., Billingsley, F., & Schwartz, I. S. (2005). Effects of video modeling alone and with self-management on compliment-giving behaviors of children with high-functioning ASD. *Journal of Positive Behavior Interventions, 7,* 33–46.

Buggey, T., Toombs, K., Gardener, P., & Cervetti, M. (1999). Training responding behaviors in students with autism: Using videotaped self-modeling. *Journal of Positive Behavior Interventions, 4,* 205–214.

Charlop, M. H., & Milstein, J. P. (1989). Teaching autistic children conversational speech using video modeling. *Journal of Applied Behavior Analysis, 22,* 275–285.

Dowrick, P. W. (1991). *Practical guide to using video in the behavioral sciences.* New York: Wiley.

Dowrick, P. W. (1999). A review of self modeling and related interventions. *Applied and Preventive Psychology, 8,* 23–39.

Haring, T. G., Kennedy, C. H., Adams, M. J., & Pitts-Conway, V. (1987). Teaching generalization of purchasing skills across community settings to autistic youth using videotape modeling. *Journal of Applied Behavior Analysis, 20,* 89–96.

Hitchcock, C. H., Dowrick, P. W., & Prater, M. A. (2003). Video self-modeling intervention in school-based settings. *Remedial and Special Education, 24,* 36–45.

Kimball, J. W., Kinney, E. M., Taylor, B. A., & Stromer, R. (2004). Video-enhanced activity schedules for children with autism: A promising package for teaching social skills. *Education and Treatment of Children, 27,* 280–298.

LeBlanc, L. A., Coates, A. M., Daneshvar, S., Charlop-Christy, M. H., Morris, C., & Lancaster, B. M. (2003). Using video modeling and reinforcement to teach perspective-taking to children with autism. *Journal of Applied Behavior Analysis, 36,* 253–257.

Mechling, L. C., Pridgen, L. S., & Cronin, B. A. (2005). Computer-based video instruction to teach students with intellectual disabilities to verbally respond to questions and make purchases in fast food restaurants. *Education and Training in Developmental Disabilities, 40,* 47–59.

Meharg, S. S., & Woltersdorf, M. A. (1990). Therapeutic use of videotape self-modeling: A review. *Advances in Behavior Research and Therapy, 12,* 85–99.

Taylor, B. A., Levin, L., & Jasper, S. (1999). Increasing play-related statements in children with autism toward their siblings: Effects of video modeling. *Journal of Developmental and Physical Disabilities, 11,* 253–264.

Richard L. Simpson is a professor of special education at the University of Kansas. He currently directs several federally supported projects to prepare teachers and leadership professionals for careers with children and youth with autism spectrum disorders. Simpson has also worked as a teacher of students with disabilities, psychologist, and administrator of several programs for students with autism. He is the former editor of the professional journal *Focus on Autism and Other Developmental Disabilities* (published by PRO-ED) and the author of numerous books and articles on autism spectrum disorders.

Jeff Sigafoos received his PhD in educational psychology from the University of Minnesota in 1990. He is currently professor of education and director of the Transforming Learning Communities Research Centre at the University of Tasmania, Australia. He is co-author of *One-to-One Training: Instructional Procedures for Learners with Developmental Disabilities* (2004) and *Enhancing Everyday Communication for Children with Disabilities* (2006).

Mark O'Reilly received his PhD in special education at the University of Illinois in 1992. He currently holds the Mollie V. Davis Professorship of Learning Disabilities in the Department of Special Education at the University of Texas at Austin. He is co-author of *Challenging Behavior and Developmental Disability* (2003) and *Behavior Analysis: Foundations and Applications to Psychology* (1999).

Berenice de la Cruz received her MA in clinical psychology at the University of Texas at El Paso in 2004. She is currently a doctoral student in the Autism and Developmental Disabilities Program at the University of Texas at Austin. She is co-author of the recent study *Comparing Video Prompting to Video Modeling for Teaching Daily Living Skills to Six Adults with Developmental Disabilities* (2005).